THE CLARINET

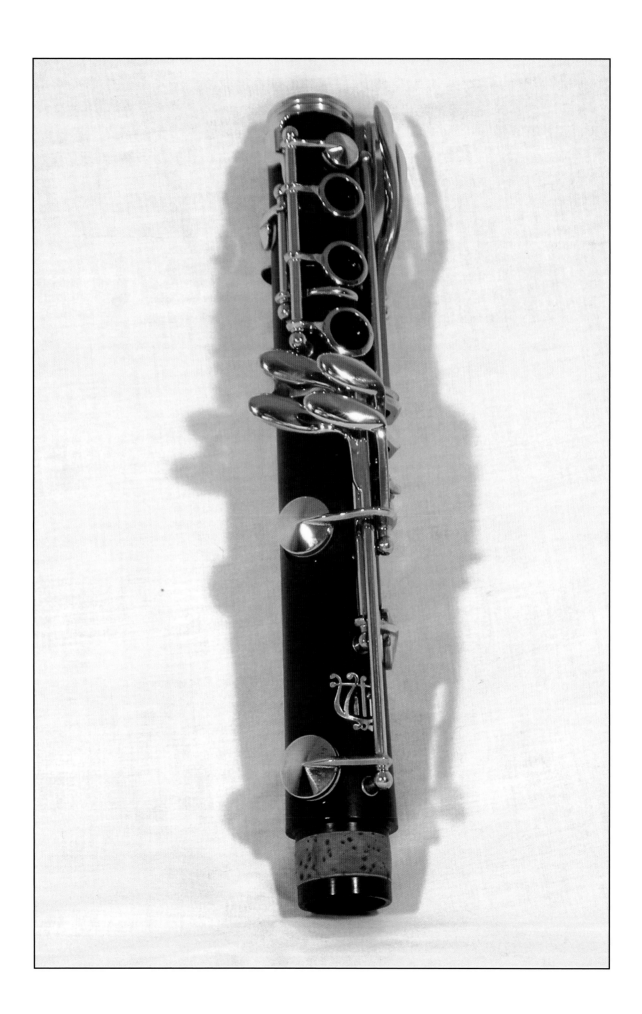

THE CLARINET

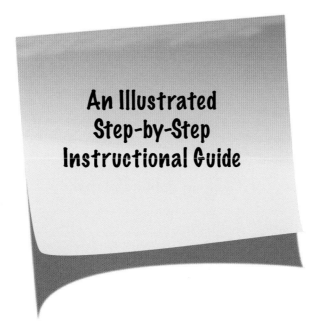

An Illustrated
Step-by-Step
Instructional Guide

Frank Cappelli

ELDORADO INK

Eldorado Ink
PO Box 100097
Pittsburgh, PA 15233
www.eldoradoink.com

First printing

1 3 5 7 9 8 6 4 2

Library of Congress Cataloging-in-Publication Data

    Cappelli, Frank.
      The clarinet / Frank Cappelli.
         p. cm. — (Learn to play)
      Includes bibliographical references (p.   ) and index.
      ISBN-13: 978-1-932904-12-3
      ISBN-10: 1-932904-12-3
      1. Clarinet—Methods. I. Title.
      MT382.C37 2007
      788.6'2193—dc22

                          2006036438

Acknowledgements

The author would like to thank all of those who provided instruments to be used in the photographs of this book, particularly Volkwein's Music of Pittsburgh (800-553-8742; www.volkweins.com) and Jerome Duepner, who provided the cover photo.

TABLE OF CONTENTS

Clarinet
Flute
Guitar
Piano
Trumpet
Violin

INTRODUCTION

The word "clarinet" comes from the Italian word *clarino* (meaning "trumpet"), with the additional suffix *-et*, meaning "little." The instrument received this name because it originally had the tone and sound of a trumpet.

An instrument called the chalumeau, the first true single reed instrument, was an ancestor of the modern clarinet. During the late 17th century, a father and son, Johann Christoph Denner and Jacob Denner, are believed to have created the clarinet by improving the chalumeau's design. They invented the register key, which gave their new instrument the ability to play more notes. The Denners also altered the shape of the mouthpiece and improved the bell.

At first, musical composers had little interest in the clarinet, preferring the simpler recorder or the chalumeau. It was not until the 18th century that Mozart and other composers began to include clarinet parts in their compositions. By 1780, the clarinet was an integral part of most orchestras and chamber music ensembles.

As the clarinet's popularity grew, the instrument continued to evolve. During the late 1700s, more keys were added and the tone holes were altered. In 1812 Iwan Müller presented a 13-keyed model that he had developed to the Paris Conservatoire, a famous musical school in Paris. The modern clarinet has seven fingerholes—six on the front and one on the back—and can play in three different registers, or ranges. These include the chalumeau (the lowest), the clarion (the middle), and altissimo (the highest).

Between 1839 and 1843 Boehm fingering, similar to the fingering method used to play the flute, was applied to the clarinet. (Boehm fingering can also be used for the saxophone and oboe, and a slight variation is used to play the bassoon.) Boehm fingering remains the primary method used today in the United States. In other countries the Oehler system is popular among clarinetists.

Today the clarinet is one of the most popular woodwind instruments. They are essential elements of all polka, military, and jazz bands, and an important part of the woodwind section of any orchestra.

There are many different kinds of clarinets—the bass clarinet, the A clarinet, the B clarinet, and E clarinet, to name a few. This book will focus on one of the most common, the Bb clarinet. Whether you are a true beginner, have a bit of musical training, or are a skilled musician on another instrument, this book's carefully developed approach can help anyone succeed in playing the clarinet.

PART ONE: Getting Started

This book is intended for the beginning clarinet player. The clarinet is an instrument that offers a variety of sounds and styles. Clarinet players can feel at home in a small jazz combo, or in a large symphony.

Anyone can play the clarinet; as with most other things in life, the level of success you will achieve depends on how much time you want to put into learning how to play.

To become a good clarinetist you need to work hard and practice. Give yourself time and always look for new ways to make yourself better. One way to do this is to listen to your favorite songs and see whether you can pick out notes or melodies that you can play on your own. Even if you can't play the entire song at first, this kind of practicing will improve your skill. Also, play with other musicians whenever you get the chance. You will learn from them as they will learn from you.

You will experience exhilaration and frustration as you learn to understand and master the clarinet. Hopefully the way this book is structured will make your experience as stress-free as possible. The instructions, diagrams, and illustrations will help you through everything from the purchase of a clarinet to playing your first songs.

1. Buying a Clarinet

When looking for an instrument, try to get the best instrument you can afford. There are a number of clarinet manufacturers to choose from. Some of the most well known are Buffet, Leblanc, Selmer, and Yamaha.

The Buffet brand is probably the most widely used by professionals. They are also expensive—about $2,000 each. They have a full, dark, and resonant tone. The only downside is that Buffet clarinets are not consistent. They can have trouble with uneven pitch, but if you get a good one, it will sound out-

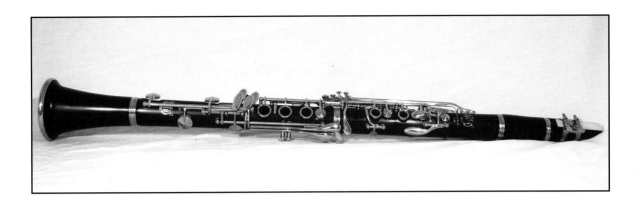

standing. If you are going to buy a Buffet, it may be worth it to ask a good clarinet player to try the instrument first to make sure it's a gem.

The Leblanc brand is the best at consistently holding pitch. They have a great feel, but they are also more expensive—about $2,400–$3,000.

The Selmer brand is the most popular with beginning students. It is very easy to hold and play. It is also much less expensive, costing hundreds, rather than thousands, of dollars.

Yamaha makes a great top-of-the-line clarinet, but the company's less expensive models suffer from irregular intonation. The tone tends to vary between the upper and lower registers, meaning that while the lower register might be in tune, the upper register might sound sharp or flat.

Go to a music store, ask questions, and try the instruments. People who work in music stores are usually musicians, and they love to talk about music. Once you've decided which brand is right for you, look at the particular instrument that you want to buy. Make sure the keys fit tightly over the holes. Anything bent will affect the sound.

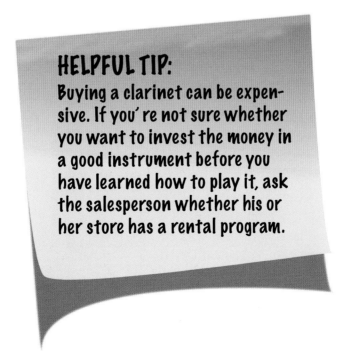

HELPFUL TIP:
Buying a clarinet can be expensive. If you're not sure whether you want to invest the money in a good instrument before you have learned how to play it, ask the salesperson whether his or her store has a rental program.

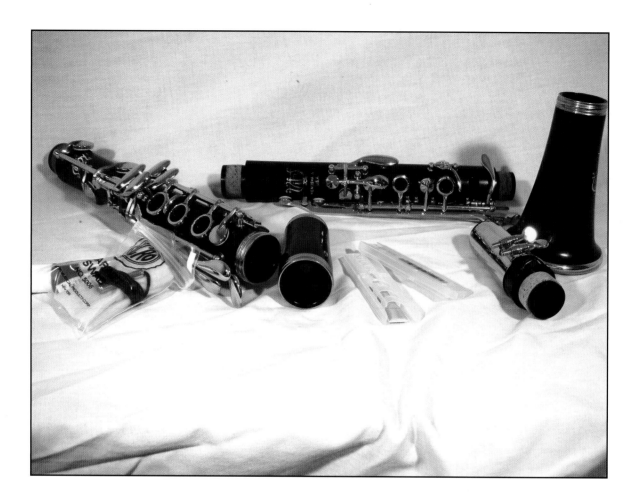

2. Parts of the Clarinet

Now that you have your clarinet, it is time to get familiar with its pieces. Make sure the case is sitting properly, so the latches open in the direction that they should, and open the case. You will see the clarinet in five pieces along with other necessary parts like reeds and cleaning cloths.

The Mouthpiece and Ligature: The mouthpiece can be made of ebonite or plastic. You attach a single reed to the mouthpiece with the metal ligature. Most reeds are made of arundo donax cane, which is a type of grass.

Reeds: The reed is what produces the sound. Clarinet reeds come in different strengths, usually soft to hard on a scale of 1-5. Most beginners use a 2 or a 2 1/2. In addition to the make and softness of the reed, the tip opening and lay of the mouthpiece also contribute to the production of a good sound.

Clarinet mouthpiece with cover

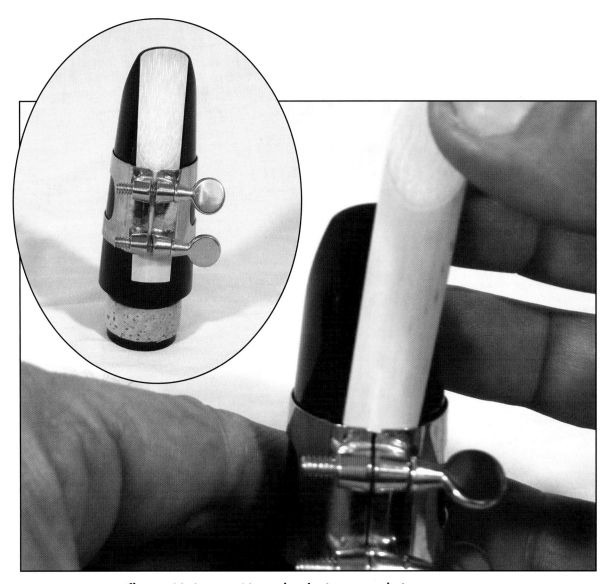

The reed is inserted into the clarinet mouthpiece

The Barrel Joint: The barrel is a short length of tube that is used to fine tune the clarinet. The tuning of the clarinet is pretty constant, but the barrel gives you an opportunity to make adjustments if needed.

The Upper Joint: The keys of the upper joint are played with your left hand. Your left thumb plays the thumb hole and register key.

The Lower Joint: The keys of the lower joint are played with your right hand. There is a cluster of keys at the bottom of the upper joint, slightly overhanging the cork of the joint. These are the trill keys, and they are also played with the right hand. Also on the lower joint is the thumb rest.

The barrel

Parts of the Clarinet

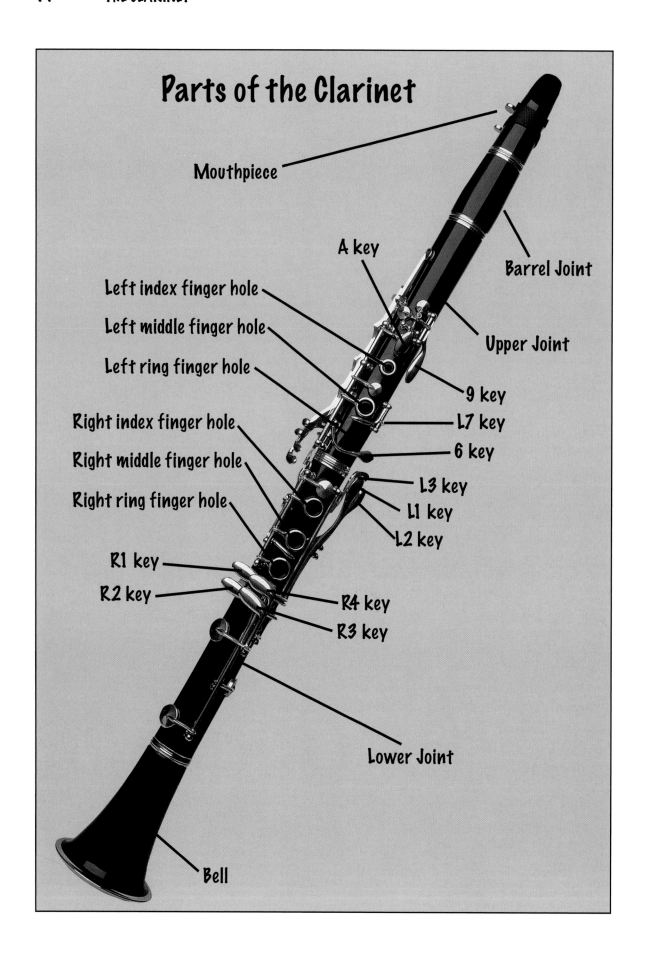

Mouthpiece

A key

Left index finger hole

Left middle finger hole

Left ring finger hole

Right index finger hole

Right middle finger hole

Right ring finger hole

R1 key

R2 key

Barrel Joint

Upper Joint

9 key

L7 key

6 key

L3 key

L1 key

L2 key

R4 key

R3 key

Lower Joint

Bell

The Bell: The bell is at the end of the instrument. The flare at the end of the bell helps to highlight the clarinet's tone, especially the lower notes.

3. Extras

In addition to your clarinet, there are a number of other items that you may want to keep in your instrument case. These will help you to take proper care of your instrument.

Reed holders, which keep the reed from becoming damaged, cost about $3 to $5. When you are done playing, gently squeeze the reed between your fingers to remove excess moisture before you put it back into the holder.

Cotton swabs are a necessity to keep in your case. You need to watch the moisture or condensation that may build up in your clarinet. Using the swab every time you play will help control this so excess moisture will not become a problem. The swabs usually come with a weighted cord or ribbon attached, which helps the cord go through the instrument.

Cork grease is used on the joints of the clarinet so that they fit together properly. The corks should fit nice and snug, but not too tight because then the clarinet is hard to take apart. Joints that are nicely lubricated are

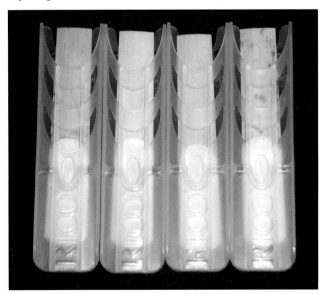

Extra reeds in a reed protector

Cotton swabs for removing moisture

The mouthpiece protector

A tube of cork grease

easier to take apart and piece together. Be careful not to use too much grease or the instrument may come apart unexpectedly when you are playing.

The mouthpiece protector, also called a cap, usually comes with all new clarinets. They are either plastic or metal. The cap should be on the clarinet whenever the instrument is not being played.

The purpose of a neck strap is to make it easier to handle the instrument. Without a neck strap, the weight of the clarinet will be on your right thumb.

4. Getting Ready to Play

The clarinet is a wind instrument, and the most important part of playing any wind instrument is learning how to breathe correctly. Clarinet players need to inhale a lot of air, and this needs to be done quickly and quietly.

Posture is important. You should stand tall with your head up and your neck and shoulders relaxed. Your weight should be equally balanced on both feet. If you are sitting, use the same posture, but sit at the front of the chair.

Imagine someone coming toward you and suddenly thrusting a finger toward your bellybutton. Your reaction would be to quickly draw in your stomach. The area that you sucked in is called your diaphragm, and those are the muscles you must use to control your breathing.

Slowly breathe in and fill that area below your stomach with air. Don't lift your shoulders, just expand your diaphragm and then slowly let the air out. As you do this, practice controlling the flow of air.

Always breathe in through your nose and out through your mouth. Practice your breathing without holding your clarinet. You can practice on just the mouthpiece. This will also help you to develop your embouchure, the muscles in your face that are needed to play the clarinet.

5. Putting your Clarinet Together

The most frequent cause of damage to the clarinet is not putting it together correctly. The keys of the clarinet are made of soft metal that can bend easily. If the keys are bent even slightly, it will change the tone of your clarinet, so be careful when putting your clarinet together.

Here are the steps you should follow when putting your instrument together:

1. Open the case on a flat surface and carefully remove each section.
2. If necessary, use the cork grease to lubricate all the cork joints, even at the mouthpiece. Make sure you cover the entire cork piece with grease. You do not have to put grease on every time, only when it becomes slightly difficult to put together. You don't want the joints to be too loose as the clarinet may then come apart as you are playing.

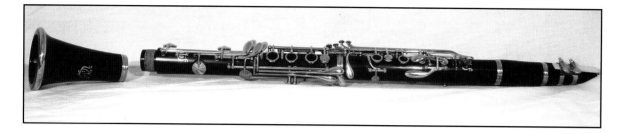

3. The lower joint is the largest piece in the case. Pick it up by its edges, not by the keys, so that you do not bend the keys. Turn the lower joint so that the two large keys and the cluster of keys are facing you. Put the palm of your right hand directly over the two large keys. If you press directly on the keys you will not hurt them. The most important thing is to keep your thumb on top of your hand and not under the clarinet. (Like when you hold a baseball bat). This keeps your thumb from damaging any key.

4. With your left hand pick up the upper joint. Wrap the fingers of your left hand around the larger of the ring keys. As you hold down the larger ring key you will see that the bridge key will lift also, they are one in the same.

5. Now that you are holding the two pieces, slide them together and slowly push them in place. Do not twist.

6. You should line up the piping. At the end of the piping is a ball. The balls should line up.

7. The bell goes on next. Hold the clarinet in your left hand and push and gently twist the bell on with your right hand.

8. Next is the barrel. Hold the clarinet in your left hand and push the barrel all the way down with your right hand.

9. When inserting the mouthpiece, turn the clarinet so the register key is facing you. Hold the clarinet with your left hand, holding the upper joint and the barrel joint. Push the mouthpiece into the barrel. The flat part of the mouthpiece should line up with the register key.

Putting on the Reed: You are almost ready to play. Get the reed wet with your mouth for about a minute. Next, place the flat side of the reed onto the flat part of the mouthpiece. Hold it in place with your thumb. Slide the ligature over the reed carefully. Do not hit the reed, as that may crack it. Slide the ligature low on the reed just passed the shaved part. Once in place, tighten the screws, as shown in the picture to the right.

You would take apart the clarinet by reversing the order above.

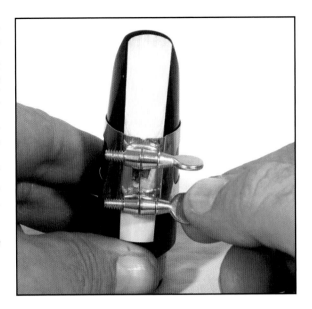

6. Cleaning

When you are finished practicing or playing, remember to use a cotton swab to clean your clarinet. Swabs made for clarinet players usually come with an attached cord or ribbon with a weight at the end. The weight helps the cord go through the instrument.

To use the swab, remove the mouthpiece and turn the clarinet upside down so the bell is facing up. Unfold the swab and run it through your hand to get it straight. Make sure there are no tangles or knots in the cord. Take the weighted end and slowly lower it into the bell until the weight comes out the other side. Do not push the swab into the bell.

Once through to the other side, turn the clarinet sideways and gently pull the swab through.

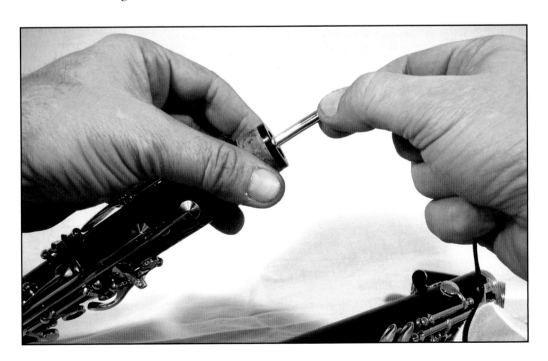

If a swab gets stuck, stop pulling immediately. Take the clarinet apart and pull the swab backwards to get it out, as shown in the photos below.

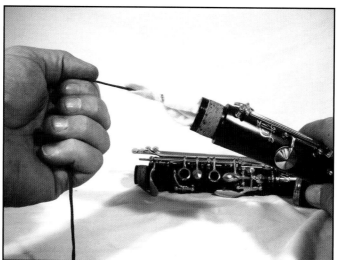

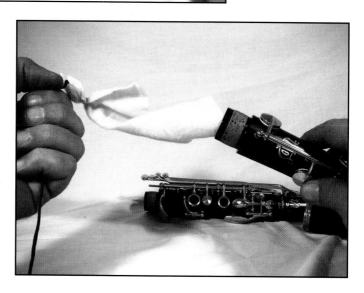

7. Holding the Clarinet

The clarinet is held in place primarily with the thumb of your right hand. As you hold the clarinet, your left hand is on top, and your right hand is on the bottom.

The fingering for the clarinet on the left hand is as follows: the thumb is H, the index finger is 1, the middle finger is 2, the ring finger is 3, and the pinky is 4. On your right hand, your index finger is 1, your middle finger is 2, your ring finger is 3, and your pinky is 4.

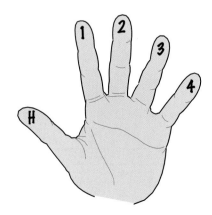

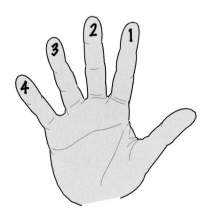

Left hand fingering   **Right hand fingering**

PART TWO: Reading Music

With what you will learn in this section, you will be able to communicate with musicians all around the world. I'll make it as painless as possible, but you've got to put in some time.

1. The Staff

The following will introduce you to some very basic concepts that will help you understand the notes on the clarinet. First, music is a language, and it is written on a staff. A staff has five lines and four spaces.

The lines and spaces are named starting at the bottom and going up, as illustrated by the staff below.

To give order to the music, the staff is divided into measures. A vertical line called a bar is used to mark out the measures. You know you're at the end of a section of music when you see a double bar line on the staff. Here is the staff with a G clef (also called a treble clef) with a 4/4 time signature and double bar line.

The double bar line tells a musician that he or she is at the end of a section or strain of music. Sometimes, however, there will be two dots before the double bar line. That means to repeat the section of music.

One other thing you may see when you are reading music is a small number at the beginning of some measures (circled in red below). This is just a helpful guide for the musician; it lets you know what measure you are playing. This can be particularly useful when you are playing music with a group and the leader or instructor wants you to start at a particular measure, rather than at the beginning of the song. Although in this book the number appears above the staff at the first measure of each line of music, in other music you may find that the number appears at the bottom of the staff, or that each measure is numbered.

Repeat Sign

2. The Notes

Next we shall take a look at what gets written on the staff. The notes tell us what tones to play and take on the names of the lines or spaces they occupy. A note has three parts.

The Head: gives a general indication of time: a hollow oval indicates a half note or a whole note, while a solid oval denotes a quarter, eighth, or other note.

The Stem: all notes except for whole notes have a stem.

The Flag: the presence of a flag indicates an eighth or sixteenth note.

The Head

The Stem

The Flag

You can find notes *on* the staff, *above* the staff, and *below* the staff.

Quarter Note

Eighth Note

Half Note

Whole Note

A quarter note has a stem and a solid oval head. It usually gets one count. If there are four beats in the measure, you might count "one, two, three, four" in your mind when playing; the quarter note would generally be played for the amount of time it takes to count "one."

An eighth note has a solid head, a stem, and a flag. Often, two eighth notes will be connected. The eighth note lasts half as long as a quarter note. So if you are mentally counting the beats in the measure, you would count "one and two and three and four and." Each of these would represent an eighth note; you would play on the "one" but not on the "and," for example.

Notes with a stem and hollow oval head are called half notes. A half note gets two counts, or beats, per measure. It is twice as long as a quarter note, so count "one, two."

A whole note is a hollow circle. It indicates a note that receives four beats.

Sometimes, you will see a dot next to a note, as shown in the lower left corner. This means that when you play the note, you need to add one-half the original value of the note to its length. For example, a dotted half note is played for three beats, while a dotted quarter note is extended by an extra eighth. (In 4/4 time each measure would have eight eighth notes; the dotted quarter note would be played for three eighths.)

Rests also appear in the measure. These symbols indicate to the musician when he or she should take a brief break from playing. Like notes, there are different symbols for rests, depending on how long the musician should be silent. Two common rests, quarter note and half note rests, are pictured below.

Dotted Half Note

Quarter Note Rest

Half Note Rest

3. Reading Musical Notes

Now that you have been introduced to reading music, it's time to take the next step. You have seen the staff, with its five lines and four spaces. You now need to learn the names of the lines and spaces of the staff. Here are the notes on the lines:

The note on the bottom line is E. The next line up is G, then B, then D, and finally F. Most students use a mnemonic device to remember the lines. They memorize the phrase:

Every **G**ood **B**oy **D**eserves **F**udge

The spaces from the bottom up are F, A, C, E. Yes, it's the word "face," which is another mnemonic that students can use to remember the notes in the spaces.

Music uses only the letters A through G, and the notes are always in alphabetical order. So if you start on the bottom line, E, the next space is F, the next line is G, and the following space is A. The next line will be B and so on. However, notes can also be written above and below the staff:

In the example above, some of the notes have an extra line or two through them, either above or below the five-line staff. These are called ledger lines, and they help the musician to easily identify the proper note.

4. Clef Symbols

In the previous section, specific notes were assigned to the lines and spaces on the staff. The way that you can be sure what note each line or space represents is to look at the beginning of the first staff of music. There, you will see a symbol called a clef. There are several different clef symbols; each indicates to the person reading the music which notes the lines and spaces on the staff represent. For the clarinet you will only need to know one, the treble, or G, clef. When you see the treble clef, you'll know that the notes on the lines are EGBDF and the notes on the spaces are FACE.

The Treble Clef

Another commonly used clef is the bass clef, but this is mostly found in piano and bass instrument music. While we won't be covering how to read bass clef in this book, it's still good to know the symbol in case you ever come across it. The lines and spaces in bass clef have different note values than the lines and spaces have in treble clef.

The Bass Clef

5. Time Signature

In addition to the clef, there is also a time signature written at the beginning of the musical staff. The time signature tells the musician how many beats are in each measure and which note is valued at one beat.

The top number indicates the number of beats per measure. So in 4/4 time, there are four beats per measure, while in 3/4 time there are three beats per measure. The bottom number tells which note gets one beat. A 4 on the bottom of the time signature means the quarter note gets one beat. In 6/8 time each measure would have 6 beats and the eighth note would be played as one beat.

Let's Review

1. Music is written on a **staff**, which has **five** lines and **four** spaces.
2. The notes of the lines are **EGBDF.**
3. The notes of the spaces are **FACE.**
4. Clarinet music is normally written in the **treble clef**.
5. The staff is divided into **measures** by vertical lines called **bar lines**.

Below are some examples of time signatures that are often used in clarinet music. You will sometimes see a C in the place of a time signature. That simply stands for 4/4, or common time. Most of the music you will see will be written either in 4/4 or 3/4 time.

2/4 Time   **4/4 Time**
(also known as common time)

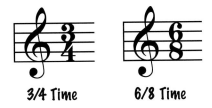

3/4 Time   **6/8 Time**

6. The Sharp and Flat Signs

The figure on the F line on the staff to the right is called a sharp. If you see it placed in front of a note, you should play the note a half step up. For example, if you see an F with the # before it, you would not play F, you would play the note a half tone higher. This note is called F#.

Notes can also be flat, which means they are played a half tone lower. A flat sign looks like a small b (pictured at left). As you've probably figured out, sharps and flats can indicate the same tone. The note G is one step above F, so you use the same fingering to play F# (a half-step up) and Gb (a half-step down). These are known as enharmonic notes.

The first place you will see flats and sharps is in the key signature. If you see one sharp in the key signature (like in the first image in this section) the music is in the key of G. If you see one flat in the key signature (as in the second image in this section), the music is in the key of F. At the top of the next page are the sharps and flats that will appear in the key signatures of some other musical keys.

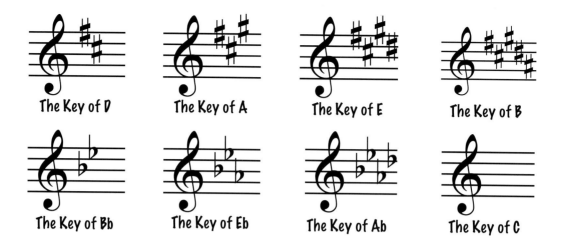

The Key of D   The Key of A   The Key of E   The Key of B

The Key of Bb   The Key of Eb   The Key of Ab   The Key of C

Sometimes a song may include a note or notes that are not in the same key as the rest of the song. When this happens, you will see a sharp or flat symbol next to the note in your music. If the note is already sharp or flat, you may see another symbol next to the note. This means to play the natural tone. Musicians call these notes "accidentals."

Natural Symbol

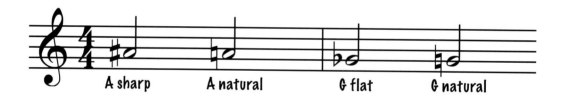

A sharp   A natural   G flat   G natural

7. Why Is the Instrument Called the Bb Clarinet?

Since we're talking about sharps and flats, you may be wondering why your clarinet is called a Bb clarinet. If you were to go to a piano and play the notes Bb, C, D, Eb, and F, they would sound like the notes C, D, E, F, and G on the clarinet. This tells you that the clarinet is tuned to a different key—in this case, Bb. Compared to the C that you would play on the piano, the C on the clarinet is actually one step down.

Sometimes this can be a problem. A beginning Bb clarinet player must be careful when reading piano, voice, or stringed instrument music. To play music written for those instruments, the clarinet player must transpose the music into the correct key and play every note one step higher.

Transposing is something that should be reserved for more advanced players, though. Most printed music for the clarinet has already been transposed for you, so you may play it as written. You will know your music is already transposed if at the very top left hand corner or next to the staff it says, "Bb clarinet."

8. Playing Your First Note (E)

The first note you will learn is the note E. To produce this note, you press the thumb key on the back of the instrument with your left thumb and use your left index finger to depress the first key. The pictures and drawing below show the proper fingering.

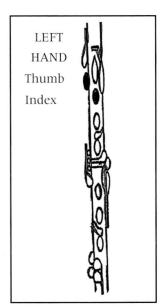

LEFT
HAND
Thumb
Index

To play the note, place the mouthpiece in your mouth and wet the reed. Place your top teeth on the mouthpiece a little less then half an inch from the end. Make a small O shape with your mouth and softly lay the reed on your lower lip. Your lower lip should sort of fold over your bottom teeth; the bottom teeth should never touch the reed. Now purse your mouth, tightening it so that no air leaks out around the mouthpiece, and blow. You should get the note E.

To start and stop a note clarinet players use their tongue. This is called tonguing. Place the clarinet back in your mouth and place the tip of your tongue over the tip of the reed. Start to blow, but keep your tongue in place. Remove your tongue, and the tone should start. This is the way to start each note on the clarinet. Once you are playing the note, put your tongue back on the tip of the reed and the sound will stop.

At right is the note E, as it would appear written in the musical staff.

The Note E

9. E Exercises

Practice playing E with these simple exercises. In the first, you will play half notes. Here, since the music is in 4/4 time, the half note is played for two beats. You'll play the note on beats one and two, and rest on three and four.

E, half notes, exercise 1

In the first six measures of the quarter note exercise below, you'll play the E on the first two beats. On the next five measures, you'll play on every beat.

E, quarter notes, exercise 1

When playing whole notes in 4/4 time, the note is held for four beats.

E, whole notes, exercise 1

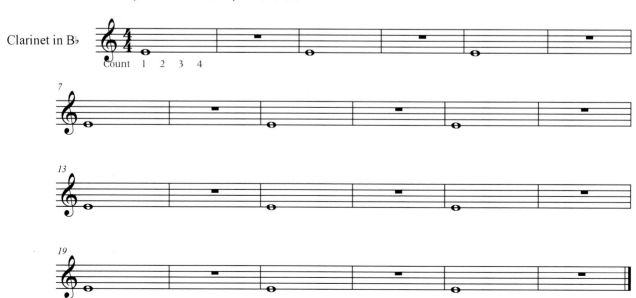

Play four eighth notes in the first two beats of each measure, and rest on the last two beats.

E, eighth notes, exercise 1

E, half notes, exercise 2

Use the following exercises to improve both your skill at producing a note clearly and cleanly, and your ability to recognize different types of notes.

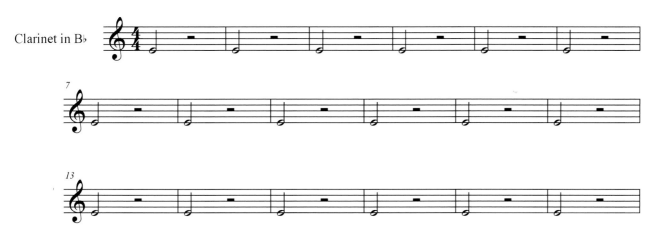

E, quarter notes, exercise 2

E, whole notes, exercise 2

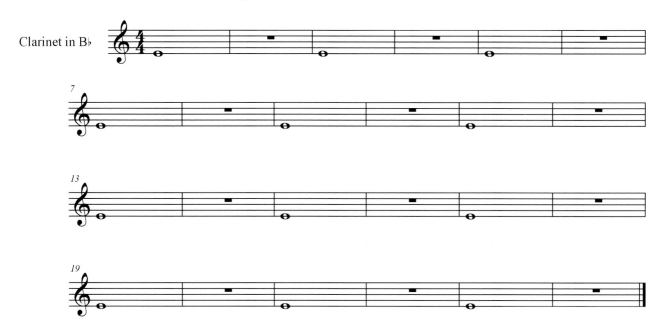

E, eighth notes, exercise 2

10. Playing the Note F

The second note you need to learn is the note F. To play this note, you only have to hold down the thumb key with your left thumb, as shown below.

The Note F

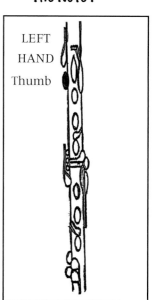

LEFT HAND Thumb

Use the following exercises to practice playing F.

F, half notes, exercise 1

F, quarter notes, exercise 1

F, whole notes, exercise 1

F, eighth notes, exercise 1

F, half notes, exercise 2

F, quarter notes, exercise 2

F, whole notes, exercise 2

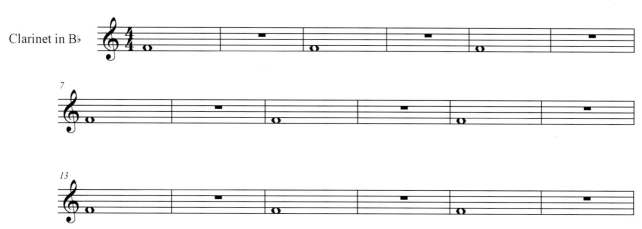

F, eighth notes, exercise 2

11. E and F Exercises

Now try switching between both notes. You should only be lifting and replacing your left index finger in order to do this.

E and F, half notes, exercise 1

E and F, quarter notes, exercise 1

E and F, whole notes, exercise 1

E and F, eighth notes, exercise 1

E and F, half notes, exercise 2

E and F, quarter notes, exercise 2

E and F, whole notes, exercise 2

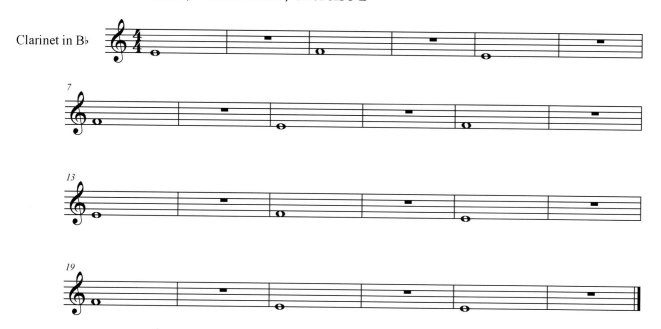

E and F, eighth notes, exercise 2

Did You Know?

Wolfgang Amadeus Mozart (1756-1791) was the first composer to include the clarinet in his orchestra.

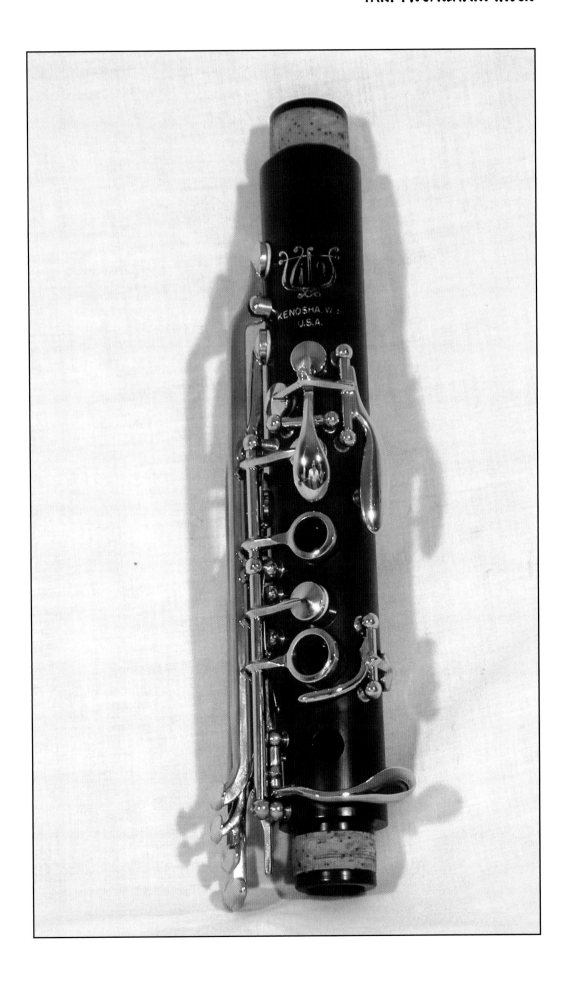

PART THREE:

Let's Play!

Now that you have gotten the feel for your clarinet and practiced playing some simple but important notes, you're ready to learn the other notes that you will need to know in order to play songs. Some of these lessons will incorporate the E and F notes you previously learned, so you will continue to practice everything we've covered.

1. The Note G

To play this G, don't press any keys; all holes are open.

The Note G

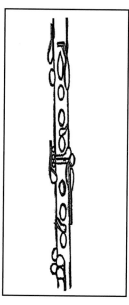

2. G Exercises

Here are some exercises you can use to practice playing the note G.

G, half notes, exercise 1

G, quarter notes, exercise 1

G, whole notes, exercise 1

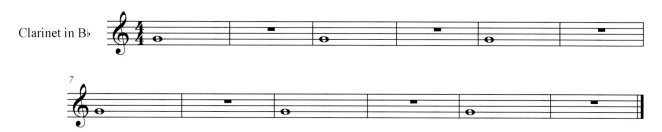

G, eighth notes, exercise 1

G, half notes, exercise 2

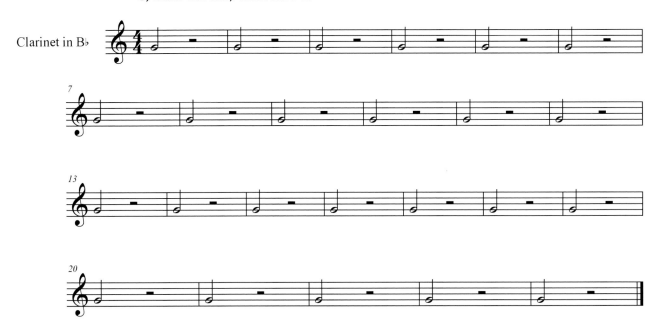

G, quarter notes, exercise 2

G, whole notes, exercise 2

G, eighth notes, exercise 2

Did You Know?

Actress Julia Roberts played the clarinet in her school band when she was growing up in Georgia.

3. Playing F and G Together

With the following exercises, you'll practice switching between the notes F and G. Remember, to play F you only have to hold down the thumb key.

F and G, half notes, exercise 1

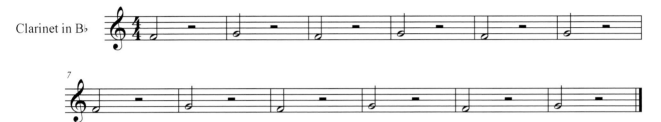

F and G, quarter notes, exercise 1

F and G, whole notes, exercise 1

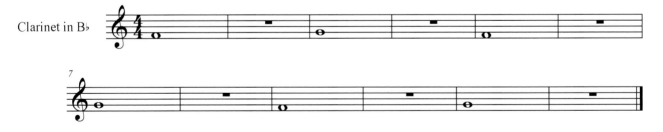

Did You Know?

Film director Woody Allen is an avid fan of jazz music and has been playing clarinet since he was a teenager. He took his stage name after one of his idols, clarinetist Woody Herman.

F and G, eighth notes, exercise 1

F and G, half notes, exercise 2

F and G, quarter notes, exercise 2

F and G, whole notes, exercise 2

Clarinet in B♭

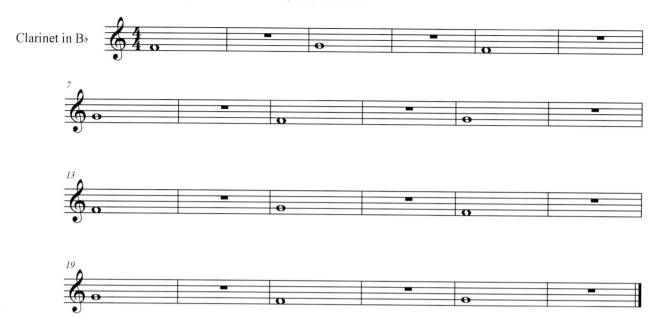

F and G, eighth notes, exercise 2

Clarinet in B♭

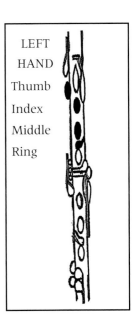

The Note Eb

4. The Note Eb

There are a number of ways to play the note Eb on a clarinet. The one pictured here uses the thumb key, first and second fingerholes, and the small L7 key below the second hole. The ring finger of your left hand should press the L7 key. You could also play E (thumb and index finger) and then cover the first lower hole with the index finger of your right hand. In some cases it may be easier to use one or the other, depending on what note you have to play next.

HELPFUL TIP:
When you sit down to practice, it can be useful to go over past lessons. This helps you refresh your memory. Eventually, playing the different notes and switching from note to note will become second nature.

5. Eb Exercises

Here are some exercises you can use to practice playing the note Eb.

Eb, half notes, exercise 1

Eb, quarter notes, exercise 1

Eb, whole notes, exercise 1

Eb, eighth notes, exercise 1

Eb, half notes, exercise 2

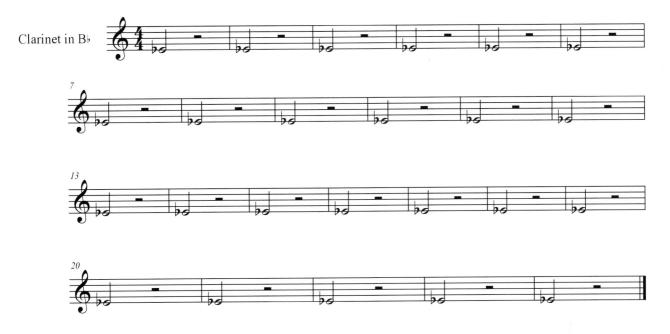

Clarinet in Bb

Eb, quarter notes, exercise 2

Clarinet in Bb

Eb, whole notes, exercise 2

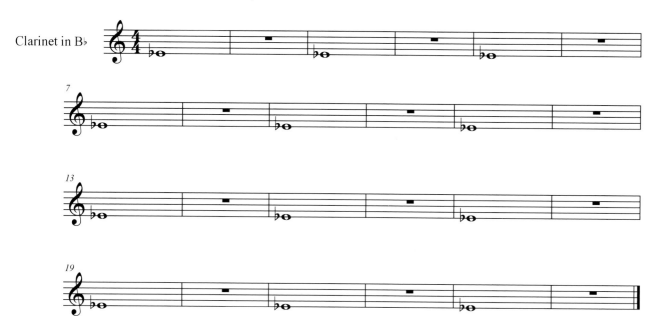

Eb, eighth notes, exercise 2

Did You Know?

Arundo Donax is the name of the plant from which clarinet reeds are made. It is more commonly referred to as the reed cane.

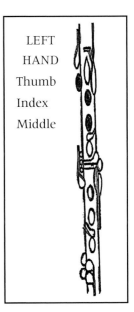

The Note D

LEFT
HAND
Thumb
Index
Middle

6. The Note D

The note D is played using your thumb on the thumb key and the first two fingers of the left hand, as shown above. Practice playing the note slowly and carefully.

7. D Exercises

Following are several pages of lessons that will help you practice playing D.

D, half notes, exercise 1

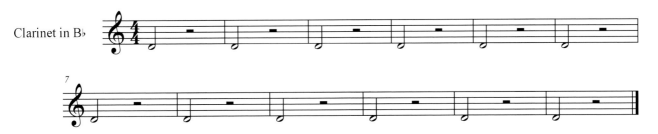

D, quarter notes, exercise 1

D, whole notes, exercise 1

D, eighth notes, exercise 1

Did You Know?

As was typical of many bandleaders of his day, Artie Shaw put together a smaller ensemble consisting of members of his big band. He named the group The Gramercy Five, after the New York City neighborhood in which he resided.

D, half notes, exercise 2

Clarinet in B♭

D, quarter notes, exercise 2

Clarinet in B♭

D, whole notes, exercise 2

Clarinet in B♭

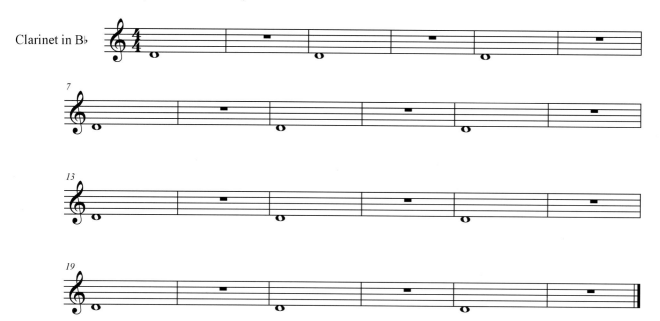

D, eighth notes, exercise 2

Clarinet in B♭

8. Playing D and E Together

Now that you've mastered D, you're ready to practice playing it with other notes. In the following lessons, you'll switch between D and E. Remember, E is played using the thumb and first finger.

D and E, half notes, exercise 1

D and E, quarter notes, exercise 1

D and E, whole notes, exercise 1

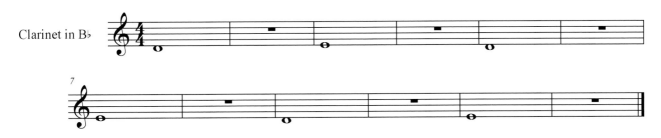

D and E, eighth notes, exercise 1

D and E, half notes, exercise 2

D and E, quarter notes, exercise 2

D and E, whole notes, exercise 2

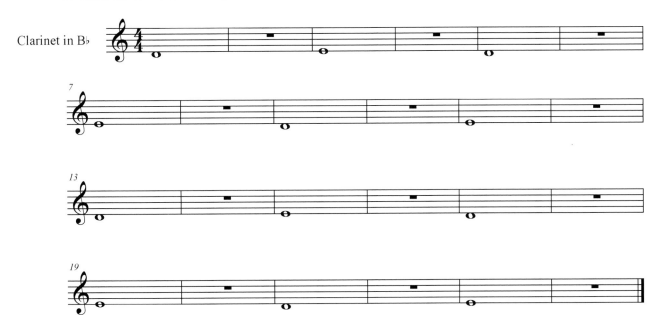

D and E, eighth notes, exercise 2

Did You Know?

A reed cane plant must be at least 1 inch (2.5 centimeters) in diameter in order to be made into reeds.

In this first song, keep your index finger and thumb pressed, and lift your middle finger on the left hand to go from D to E.

Your First Song

Clarinet in B♭

9. The Note Middle C

Middle C is played using the thumb key and first three fingers.

The Note Middle C

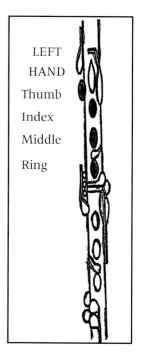

LEFT
HAND
Thumb
Index
Middle
Ring

10. Middle C Exercises

Here are some exercises you can use to practice playing the note Middle C.

Middle C, half notes, exercise 1

Middle C, quarter notes, exercise 1

Middle C, whole notes, exercise 1

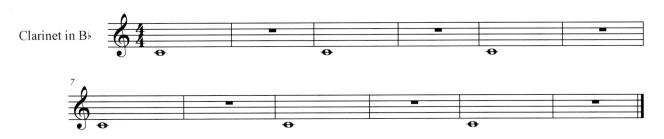

Middle C, eighth notes, exercise 1

Middle C, half notes, exercise 2

Middle C, quarter notes, exercise 2

Did You Know?

Director Steven Spielberg can be seen playing clarinet in an orchestra during a scene at the beginning of his 1975 film *Jaws*.

Middle C, whole notes, exercise 2

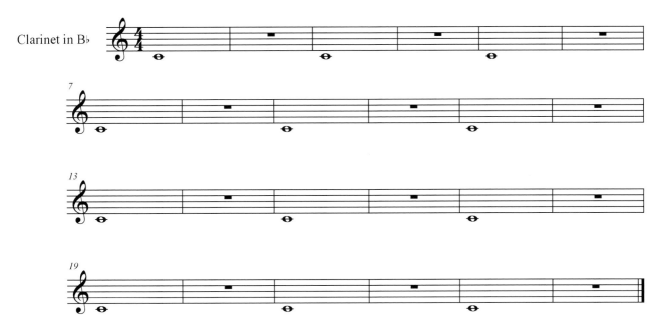

Middle C, eighth notes, exercise 2

11. The Notes C and D

Now let's try combining the notes that you've learned. First practice switching between middle C and D.

Middle C and D, half notes

Middle C and D, quarter notes

Middle C and D, whole notes

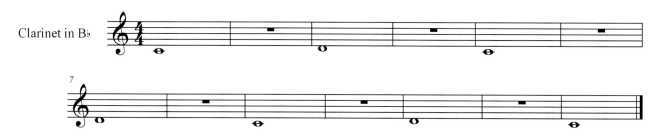

Middle C and D, eighth notes

12. The Notes C Through G

Now try playing all the notes you've learned so far. Once you've mastered these exercises, you'll be ready to play some simple songs.

Middle C through G, half notes, exercise 1

Middle C through G, quarter notes, exercise 1

Middle C through G, whole notes, exercise 1

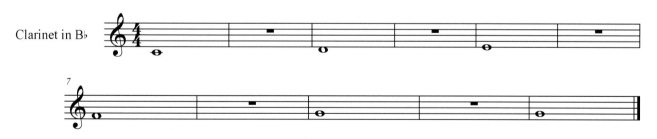

Middle C through G, eighth notes, exercise 1

Middle C through G, half notes, exercise 2

Middle C through G, quarter notes, exercise 2

Middle C through G, whole notes, exercise 2

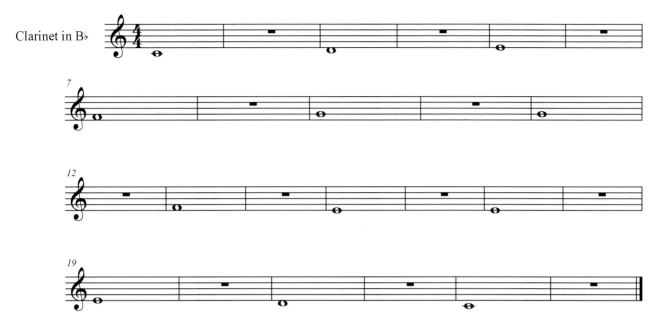

Middle C through G, eighth notes, exercise 2

13. Playing Dotted Notes

In the next three songs, you will see a small dot to the right of some notes. These are called dotted notes; you may recall that they were discussed on page 24. When you see a dotted note, you must extend the length of time that note is played by one-half of its original value.

In the song "Play with the Dots," the dotted notes are all half notes; they appear in the second, fourth, eighth, and twelfth measures. In 4/4 time, a half note ordinarily gets two beats. Half of that is one beat, so a dotted half note is held for a total of three beats.

Play with the Dots

The song "Bring the Threes" is in 3/4 time, which means there are three beats in each measure. The value of the half note is still two beats, so the dotted half note is once again played for a total of three beats. Therefore, the dotted half notes in measures two, four, six, seven, eight, nine, ten, and twelve are played for the entire measure.

Bring the Threes

Watch for dotted half notes in this well-known song.

When the Saints Go Marching In

Traditional

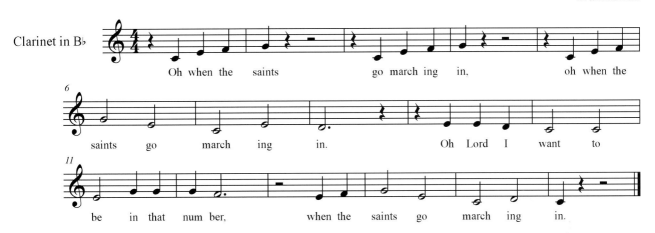

DID YOU KNOW?

The first version of the song "When the Saints Go Marching In" was published in 1896. The music was written by James Milton Black, while the original lyrics were credited to Katharine Purvis. However, there have been many different variations of the lyrics.

Although "When the Saints Go Marching In" is a Christian hymn that often appears in church songbooks, it has also been a Dixieland jazz standard for nearly a century. The song is closely identified with the city of New Orleans, where the Dixieland style of jazz developed in the early 20th century. A distinctive feature of the Dixieland sound is that one instrument (usually the trumpet) plays the melody of the song (or a slight variation), while the other musicians (usually playing guitar or banjo, string bass or tuba, piano, and drums) improvise around that melody.

During the 1930s, the famous trumpeter Louis Armstrong hit the pop charts with his recording of the song. Many other singers have recorded or performed the song as well, including Judy Garland, Fats Domino, Jerry Lee Lewis, The Beatles, Elvis Presley, and Bruce Springsteen.

14. Playing Staccato Notes

In the following songs, you will notice a dot below some of the notes. This dot indicates that the notes should be played abruptly; there should be a distinct silence between each note, although the rhythm of the measure should not change. This is called playing staccato.

Your tongue is the key to playing staccato notes on the clarinet. Use the tip of your tongue to stop the note abruptly. Try the technique when playing the song "Mambo Mambo."

Mambo Mambo

When playing "Jingle Bells," be careful not to confuse the staccato notes with the dotted notes!

"Jingle Bells" also introduces something new: a repeat sign at the end of the eighth measure. When you reach the repeat sign, go back to the beginning and play the music over. The horizontal line above measures seven and eight (marked with a 1) indicate that these measures will be replaced the second time through. During the second playing, after measure six you should jump to the second ending (marked with a 2) and play the last two measures.

Jingle Bells

Traditional

Remember, when the stems of the notes are pointing down, the dot indicating that the music should be played staccato appears above the note.

15. Slurring Your Music

A curved line above or below several notes (depending on whether the stems are pointing up or down) indicates that they are to be played without separation, or slurred. When playing a clarinet, this means that you should not use your tongue to clearly articulate each note.

In the exercise below, play the slurred notes smoothly. Try to play all of the slurred notes in one breath, without taking a break.

Slurring your music

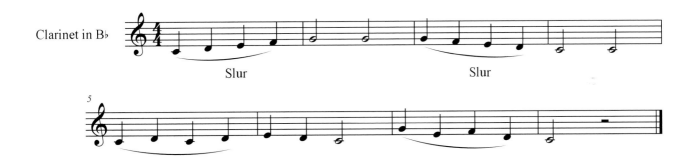

In "The Drinking Song," you'll be playing both staccato and slurred notes.

The Drinking Song

German

When reading music, be careful not to confuse the slur mark with a tie, which is also a curved line. The tie links two notes of the same pitch to show that they should be played without a break.

The Note A

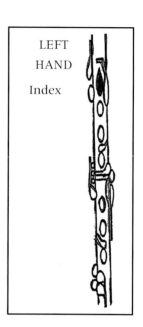

LEFT
HAND
Index

16. The Note A

Playing the note A requires using a new key, the A key, which is located above the top hole on the clarinet. The note is not hard to play. Rock your index finger up to hit this key, while uncovering the thumb hole. You do not need to pick up your entire finger to hit the key.

Did You Know?

The wood used to make clarinets comes from the Mpingo tree, which is found only in Africa. Although it is expensive, the dense composition of the wood makes it an ideal resonator.

17. A Exercises

Here are some exercises you can use to practice playing the note A.

A, half notes, exercise 1

A, quarter notes, exercise 1

A, whole notes, exercise 1

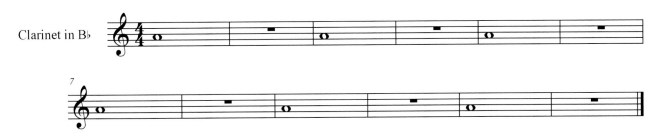

A, eighth notes, exercise 1

A, half notes, exercise 2

Clarinet in B♭

A, quarter notes, exercise 2

Clarinet in B♭

A, whole notes, exercise 2

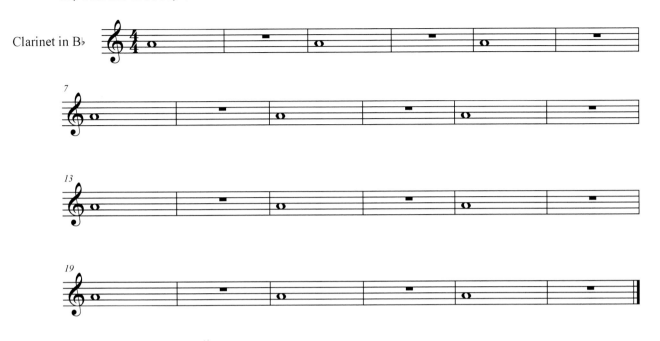

A, eighth notes, exercise 2

18. The Note Bb and Exercises

To play Bb, start with the fingering for A. Now press down the register key on the back of the clarinet with your thumb (pictured). This is Bb. With the addition of this note you will be able to play a new song!

The Note Bb

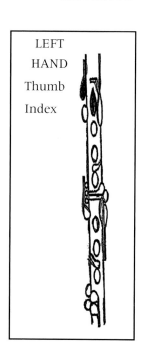

LEFT
HAND
Thumb
Index

Bb, half notes, exercise 1

Bb, quarter notes, exercise 1

Bb, whole notes, exercise 1

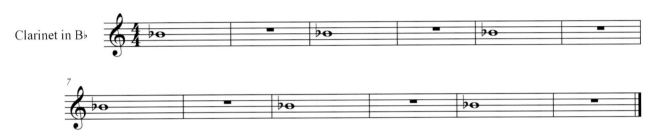

Bb, eighth notes, exercise 1

Bb, half notes, exercise 2

Bb, quarter notes, exercise 2

Bb, whole notes, exercise 2

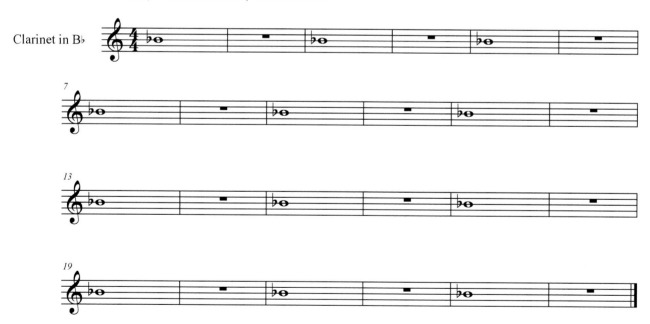

Bb, eighth notes, exercise 2

Aura Lee

Traditional

19. The Note B and Exercises

For this note we are going to introduce some new keys. There are a number of ways to play a B. The one in the diagram here requires both back keys to be pressed (you can do this with your left thumb), as well as all six holes. With your left pinky, hit the largest key in the cluster of three keys down the left side of the clarinet. With your right pinky, press the bottom inside key of the cluster of four keys at the bottom of the clarinet. Make sure that your left thumb still covers the tone hole.

The Note B

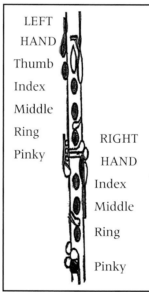

B, half notes, exercise 1

B, quarter notes, exercise 1

B, whole notes, exercise 1

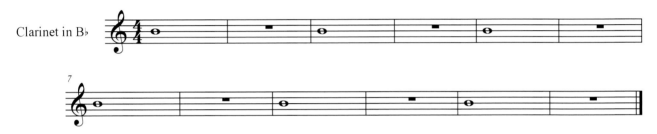

B, eighth notes, exercise 1

B, half notes, exercise 2

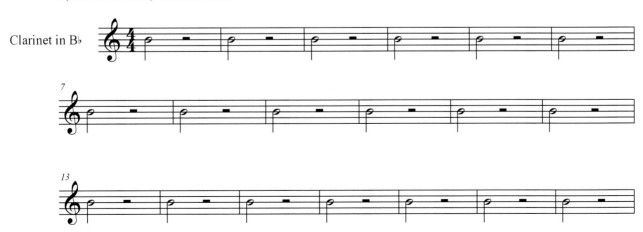

B, quarter notes, exercise 2

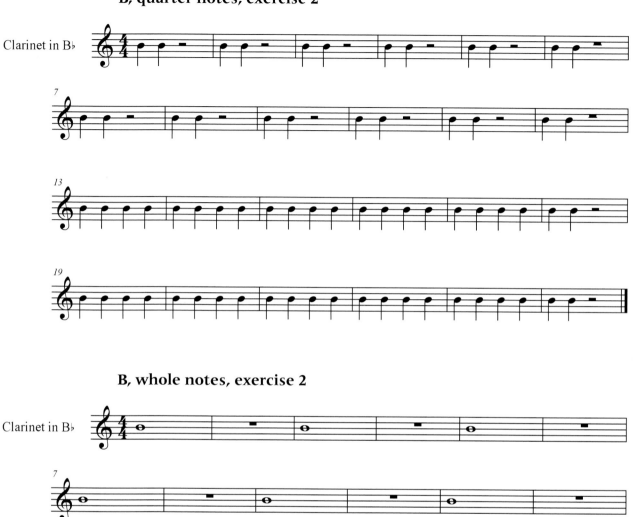

B, whole notes, exercise 2

B, eighth notes, exercise 2

20. The Note Upper C

Start with the fingering for B from the previous lesson. Now, lift your left pinky. This is the fingering for Upper C.

The Note Upper C

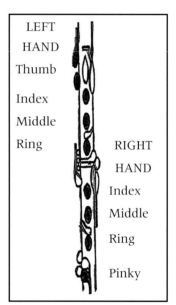

HELPFUL TIP:
The higher the note, the more difficult it will be to play with a pleasing sound. Keep practicing the high notes until you can produce a clear tone.

21. Upper C Exercises

Here are some exercises you can use to practice playing the note Upper C.

Upper C, half notes, exercise 1

Upper C, quarter notes, exercise 1

Upper C, whole notes, exercise 1

Upper C, eighth notes, exercise 1

Upper C, half notes, exercise 2

Upper C, quarter notes, exercise 2

Did You Know?

Although modern clarinetists now use reeds that are factory-made, in the past they used to make their own.

Upper C, whole notes, exercise 2

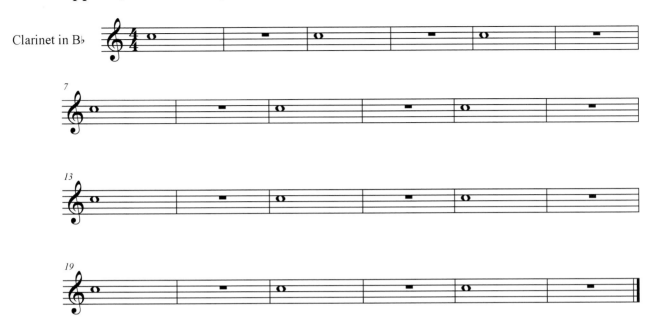

Upper C, eighth notes, exercise 2

22. The Note Upper D

To play the Upper D, press both back keys with your left thumb and cover all six finger holes.

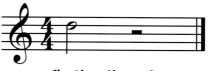

The Note Upper D

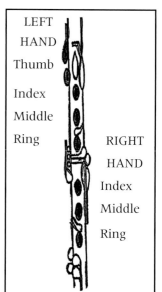

LEFT HAND

Thumb

Index

Middle

Ring

RIGHT HAND

Index

Middle

Ring

23. Upper D Exercises

Here are some exercises you can use to practice playing the note Upper D.

Upper D, half notes, exercise 1

Clarinet in B♭

Upper D, quarter notes, exercise 1

Upper D, whole notes, exercise 1

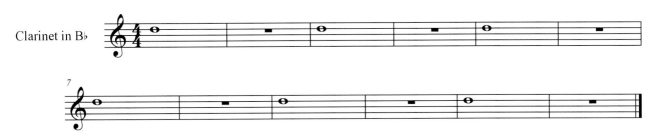

Upper D, eighth notes, exercise 1

Upper D, half notes, exercise 2

Upper D, quarter notes, exercise 2

Upper D, whole notes, exercise 2

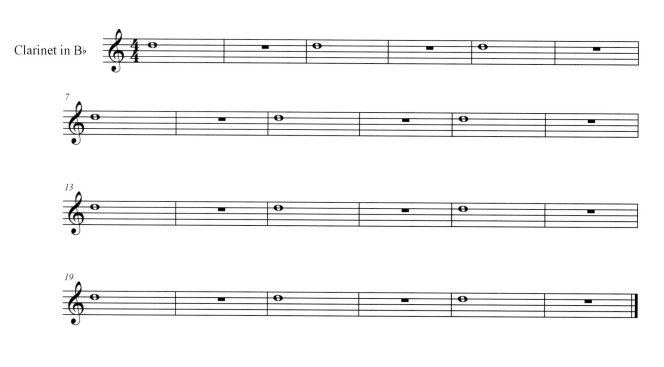

Upper D, eighth notes, exercise 2

Clarinet in B♭

Did You Know?

Aside from being a virtuoso clarinet player and having a lucrative career as a bandleader, Benny Goodman was responsible for helping end racial segregation in the United States. He was the first big-name bandleader to hire African-American musicians.

24. The Note Upper E

To move from the Upper D to Upper E, lift the ring finger on your right hand.

The Note Upper E

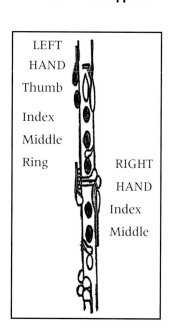

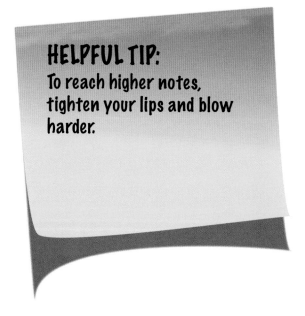

HELPFUL TIP:
To reach higher notes, tighten your lips and blow harder.

25. Upper E Exercises

Here are some exercises you can use to practice playing the note Upper E.

Upper E, half notes, exercise 1

Upper E, quarter notes, exercise 1

Upper E, whole notes, exercise 1

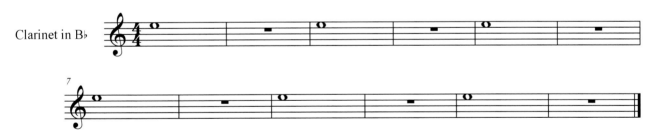

Upper E, eighth notes, exercise 1

Upper E, half notes, exercise 2

Upper E, quarter notes, exercise 2

Upper E, whole notes, exercise 2

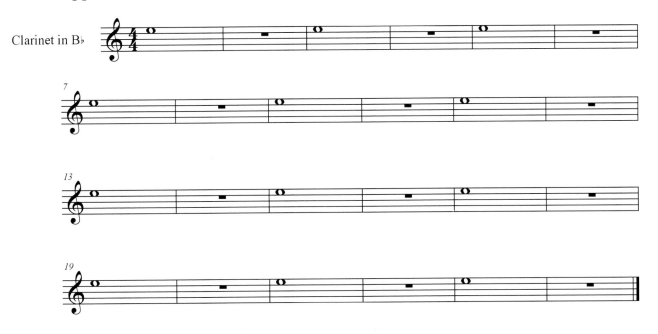

Upper E, eighth notes, exercise 2

Did You Know?

The largest clarinet ever made is called the BBBb Octocontrabass Clarinet. There is only one in existence and its range goes to the lowest Bb note on the piano keyboard.

26. The Note Upper F and Exercises

For the Upper F, cover the back two keys, all three holes for the left hand, and the first hole for the right hand.

The Note Upper F

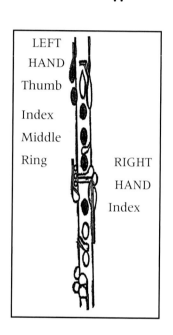

LEFT HAND
Thumb

Index
Middle
Ring

RIGHT HAND
Index

Upper F, half notes, exercise 1

Clarinet in B♭

Upper F, quarter notes, exercise 1

Upper F, whole notes, exercise 1

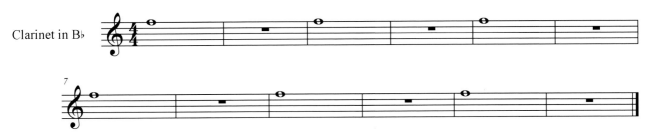

Upper F, eighth notes, exercise 1

Upper F, half notes, exercise 2

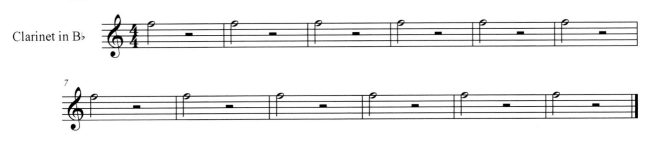

Upper F, quarter notes, exercise 2

Upper F, whole notes, exercise 2

Did You Know?

Every Monday night Woody Allen can be found playing clarinet at Michael's Pub in New York City.

Upper F, eighth notes, exercise 2

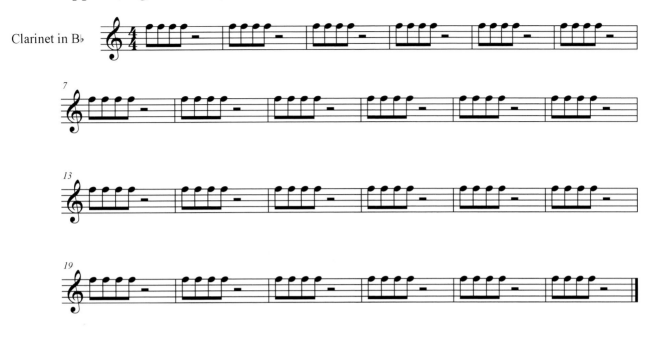

27. Songs

Here are some simple but popular songs; use them to practice or play them for your family or friends.

Mary Had a Little Lamb

Folk

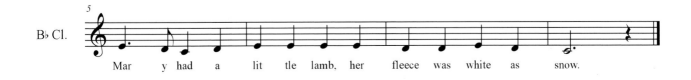

When Johnny Comes Marching Home

Traditional

Clarinet in B♭

When John ny comes march ing home a gain, hu rah____ hu rah.____

When John ny comes march ing home a gain,____ hu rah, hu rah.

The__ men will sing, and the girls will shout. The la dies they will all turn out,

and we'll all feel gay when John ny comes march ing home.____

"When Johnny Comes Marching Home" was one of the most popular songs during the American Civil War (1861-65).

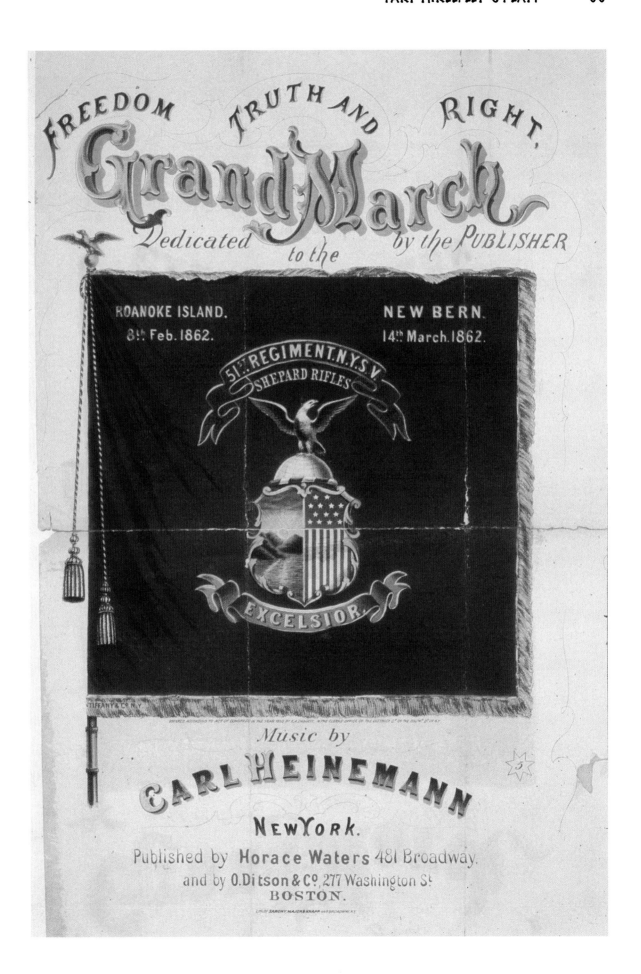

The Gospel Train

Spiritual

Clarinet in B♭

The gos pel train is com in' I hear it just at

B♭ Cl.

hand I hear the wheels a mov in' and rum blin' through the

B♭ Cl.

la nd Get on board, lit tle chil ren get on board, lit tle

B♭ Cl.

chil dren get on board, lit tle chil dren there's room for ma ny more

Did You Know?

Usually, an orchestra playing classical music will include at least two clarinetists. Each player is typically equipped with two clarinets, one in Bb and the other in A. Some 19th century composers expanded the clarinet section to as many as nine players.

Good King Wenceslas

Traditional European

Clarinet in B♭

Good King Wen ces las looked out on the feast of Ste phen,

B♭ Cl.

when the snow lay round a bout, deep and crisp, and e ven.

B♭ Cl.

Bright ly shone the moon that night, though the frost was cru el,

B♭ Cl.

when a poor man came in sight, gath' ring win ter fu el.

Blow the Man Down

American

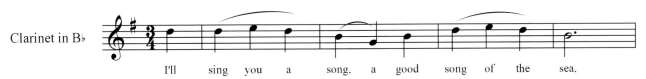

Clarinet in B♭

I'll sing you a song, a good song of the sea,

B♭ Cl.

way hey, blow the man down. Come on and join in, sing a

B♭ Cl.

chor us with me. Give me some time to blow the man down.

APPENDIX: Finding the Notes

Regardless of which instrument a student of music is learning, a diagram of the keys of the piano offers one of the best illustrations of how most western music is organized. Comprehending the relationship between different notes gives a clarinet player both a greater understanding of his or her instrument and a grasp of the basics of music theory.

Typically, a modern piano has around 88 keys. As you can see in the diagram on the opposite page, these keys are colored either black or white and repeat a specific pattern throughout the keyboard. That is, with the exception of the extreme left of the keyboard (the lowest notes) and the extreme right (the highest notes), you will find groupings of three white keys with two black keys between them and four white keys with three black keys between them. Each of these keys is given a name corresponding to the letters of the alphabet A through G. The letter names are assigned to the white, and the black keys' names are letters with either a sharp sign or flat sign after them.

The pitch that sounds when you strike the white key immediately to the left of the grouping of two black keys is known as C. Depending upon the number of keys on the piano being played, this note will reoccur six or seven times throughout the instrument. The frequency of each C is twice that of the C immediately to its left and one-half that of the C to its right. Because of this special relationship, these notes sound very similar to our ears, hence, the reason why they have the same name. The interval between these adjacent pitches with the same name is known as an octave, and this relationship is true for all similarly named notes found on the keyboard.

In order to clear up confusion caused by the fact that there are as many as 88 notes (maybe more) on a piano and many fewer note names, musicians, over time, have developed a way to differentiate between the notes that have the same name. Beginning with the C note found farthest to the left of the keyboard, a number is added to the note name indicating the octave in which the note occurs. For example, the first C that appears on the

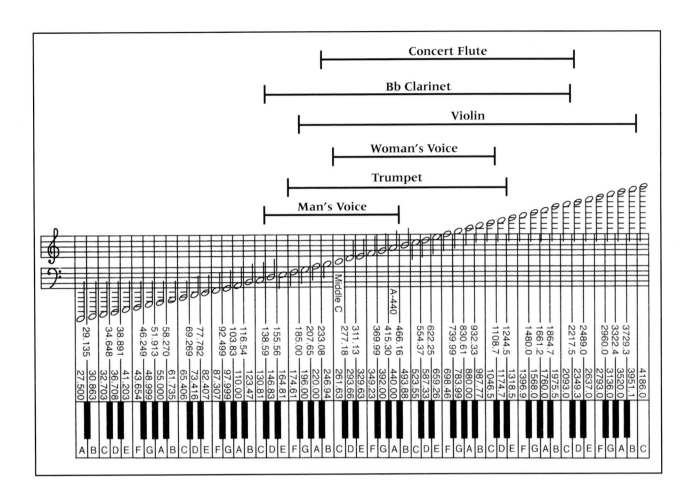

keyboard is known as "C1," the D that appears next to that is known as "D1," and so on. Middle C is also known as C4. Depending upon the piano's manufacturer, you may find that there is a different number of notes to the left of the first C on the keyboard. Since these notes do not comprise a complete octave, the number zero follows their letter name.

You'll notice that there are eleven keys between notes of the same name. Each of these keys represents a change in pitch of one half step. It can then be concluded that an octave covers a distance of 12 half steps, or six whole steps.

CLARINET TIMELINE

2700 B.C.: The Egyptians create a single-reed, double-bore instrument called the zummara.

A.D. 200: Recorders evolve from their early Iron Age incarnations. They have seven holes and a solid whistle shape to produce sound.

1600s: Baroque recorders are invented. Although the design allowed for a two octave range, they are really only reliable over a range of about an octave and a fifth.

mid-1600s: The baroque chalumeau is invented, an instrument that introduces a single reed to the body of a recorder. There were four types, ranging from treble to bass, and they had six to eight finger holes.

1690-1710: Johann Christoph Denner of Nuremberg and his son Jacob develop the register key, which allows the clarinet to play a greater range of notes.

1712: The earliest known works for the clarinet are composed, a set of duets by French composer Estienne Roger.

1716: Antonio Vivaldi writes the earliest known examples of orchestral use of the clarinet in his oratorio *Juditha Triumphans*.

1789: Wolfgang Amadeus Mozart writes "Clarinet Quintet in A Major." One of the earliest works written specifically for the instrument, it marks the first time that the clarinet is fully incorporated into a chamber music ensemble.

Wolfgang Amadeus Mozart

1812:   Iwan Müller invents new pads for the clarinet. Previously, the pads (made from leather or felt strips) leaked air, so they were not used extensively. The new pads, made of leather or gut and stuffed with wool, permitted Müller to add more keys to the clarinet, bringing the total number to 13.

1818:   The first metal clarinet is produced.

1823:   César Janssen of the Paris Opera invents "roller keys," allowing the clarinetist to slide from one key to another.

1833:   Johannes Brahms is born in Hamburg, Germany. Along with trio and quintet pieces for clarinet, it is also noteworthy that Brahms composed two sonatas for clarinet with piano accompaniment.

1839:   Hyacinthe Klosé and Louis-August Buffet introduce the design of the modern clarinet. The Klosé-Buffet design innovated the use of "moveable rings" around the tone holes and had seventeen keys and six rings, as do present-day instruments.

1869:   The first machine-made reeds are produced.

Early 1900s: Dr. R. H. Stein, a Berlin musicologist, makes the most successful quarter-tone clarinet. The quarter-tone clarinet was, however, abandoned.

1909:   Clarinetist Benny Goodman is born in Chicago. Known as "King of Swing," "Patriarch of the Clarinet," "The Professor," and "Swing's Senior Statesman," he was a virtuoso on the clarinet and arguably the best jazz clarinetist of the 20th century.

1910s: Clarinet becomes a huge part of the jazz movement in the United States. Dixieland Jazz grows out of New Orleans, Chicago Jazz began to develop, and in the northeast a "hot" style of ragtime becomes popular.

1930:   Plastic and plexiglas mouthpieces are first manufactured.

1952:   The S-K mechanism is developed. This allows separate holes and keys for a register key and a resonance key for the note B-flat, resulting in better tuned thirds and a better sounding altissimo register.

2004:   Artie Shaw dies in California. Shaw was an innovative bandleader and a master clarinetist. At the height of his popularity he earned $30,000 per week—quite impressive, considering the fact that this was during the Great Depression.

INTERNET RESOURCES

http://www.menc.org/

The National Association for Music Education is an organization whose mission is to "advance music education by encouraging the study and making of music by all." Go to this site for more information and articles related to issues in music education, making a donation, and how you can become a member.

http://musiced.about.com/od/beginnersguide/bb/buyclarinet.htm

At this website you'll find a list of helpful tips for buying your first clarinet.

http://www.ibreathemusic.com/

An invaluable resource for any musician, this site has forums and articles covering a wide range of music-related topics, including composition, improvisation, and ear training.

http://www.zacharymusic.com/Zachary_Music/ClcarePics.htm

Here you'll see a highly informative article describing, in detail, how to care for your clarinet. High quality color photos illustrate each step of the process.

http://www.jazzreview.com/

An excellent website for everything associated with jazz. Here you'll find CD and concert reviews, interviews with numerous musicians, and dozens of jazz-related articles.

http://www.bennygoodman.com/
This is the official site of "The King of Swing," maintained by Benny Goodman's estate.

http://www.8notes.com/
A great resource for all musicians, this site has clarinet sheet music for 55 songs available for free download, along with fingering charts, a glossary of music terms, an online metronome, and links to other useful music websites.

http://www.clarinet.org
The International Clarinet Association's website is dedicated to "collaborating on the artistry, technique, teaching, and physics of our wonderful instrument."

http://www.classical.com/
Though a small fee is charged for subscription, this site offers listening, downloads, custom CDs, and a huge resource of entertaining information to expand your classical music knowledge.

http://www.woodwind.org/clarinet/index.html
Here you'll find various resources, bulletin boards, chat rooms, and lots of other valuable tools for clarinet players of all age and skill levels.

http://www.woodwind.org/clarinet/Study/FingeringCharts/bbfinger.html
This online fingering chart uses photos and graphics to illustrate how to play different notes on the clarinet.

GLOSSARY

Accidental—a sharp, flat, or natural note that occurs in a piece of music but is not indicated in the key signature.

Bar lines—these vertical lines mark the division between measures of music.

Beat—the pulse of the music, which is usually implied using the combination of accented and unaccented notes throughout the composition.

Chord—three or more different tones played at the same time.

Clef (bass and treble)—located on the left side of each line of music, these symbols indicate the names and pitch of the notes corresponding to their lines and spaces.

Eighth note—a note with a solid oval, a stem, and a single tail that has 1/8 the value of a whole note.

Embouchure—the adjustment of the lips and tongue in playing a woodwind instrument.

Enharmonic notes—notes that are written differently in a musical score, but have the same pitch when played (for example, F# and Gb).

Flat sign (b)—a symbol that indicates that the note following it should be lowered by one half step. This remains in effect for an entire measure, unless otherwise indicated by a natural sign.

Half note—a note with a hollow oval and stem that has 1/2 the value of a whole note.

Half step—a unit of measurement in music that is the smallest distance between two notes, either ascending or descending. An octave is divided equally into 12 half steps.

Interval—the distance in pitch between two tones, indicated using half and whole steps.

Key signature—found between the clef and time signature, it describes which notes to play with sharps or flats throughout a piece of music.

Measure—a unit of music contained between two adjacent bar lines.

Music staff—the horizontal lines and spaces between and upon which music is written.

Natural sign—a symbol which instructs that a note should not be played as a sharp or a flat.

Notes—written or printed symbols which represent the frequency and duration of tones contained in a piece of music.

Octave—a relationship between two pitches where one tone has double (or half) the frequency of the other.

Pitch—the perceived highness or lowness of a sound or tone.

Quarter note—a note with a solid oval and a stem that is played for 1/4 of the duration of a whole note.

Repeat sign—a pair of vertical dots that appear near bar lines that indicate a section of music that is to be played more than once.

Rest—a figure that is used to denote silence for a given duration in a piece of music.

Scale—a sequence of notes in order of pitch in ascending or descending order.

Sharp sign (#)—this symbol indicates that the note following it should be raised by one half-step. This remains in effect for an entire measure, unless otherwise indicated by a natural sign.

Tempo—the speed at which music is to be played. It is notated by either a word describing the relative speed of the piece or by the number of beats per minute (B.P.M.) that occur as it is played.

Time signature—located to the right of the clef and key signatures, the top digit indicates the number of beats per measure, and the number at the bottom shows which kind of note receives one beat.

Tone—a distinct musical sound which can be produced by a voice or instrument.

Whole note—a note indicated by a hollow oval without a stem. It has the longest time value and represents a length of 4 beats when written in 4/4 time.

Whole step—a unit of measurement in music that is equal to two half steps.

INDEX

ABOUT THE AUTHOR

Frank Cappelli is a warm, engaging artist, who possesses the special ability to transform the simple things of life into a wonderful musical experience. He has had an impressive career since receiving a B.A. in music education from West Chester State College (now West Chester University). Frank has performed his music at many American venues—from Disney World in Florida to Knott's Berry Farm in California—as well as in Ireland, Spain, France, and Italy. He has also performed with the Detroit Symphony, the Buffalo Philharmonic, the Pittsburgh Symphony, and the Chattanooga Symphony.

In 1987, Frank created Peanut Heaven, a record label for children. The following year, he worked with WTAE-TV in Pittsburgh to develop *Cappelli and Company*, an award winning children's television variety show. The weekly program premiered in 1989, and is now internationally syndicated.

In 1989, Frank signed a contract with A&M Records, which released his four albums for children (*Look Both Ways, You Wanna Be a Duck?, On Vacation,* and *Good*) later that year. *Pass the Coconut* was released by A&M in 1991. *Take a Seat* was released in September of 1993. With the 1990 A&M Video release of *All Aboard the Train and Other Favorites* and *Slap Me Five*, Cappelli's popular television program first became available to kids nationwide. Both videos have received high marks from a number of national publications, including *People Magazine, Video Insider, Billboard, USA Today, Entertainment Weekly* and *TV Guide*.

Frank has received many awards, including the Parent's Choice Gold Award, regional Emmy Awards, the Gabriel Award for Outstanding Achievement in Children's Programming, and the Achievement in Children's Television Award. He is a three-time recipient of the Pennsylvania Association of Broadcasters' award for Best Children's Program in Pennsylvania.